ON THE FARM

FROM FARM TO TABLE

Warren Singer

Enslow PUBLISHING

Published in 2026 by Enslow Publishing, LLC
2544 Clinton Street
Buffalo, NY 14224

First Published 2025 by Redback Publishing

Author: Warren Singer
Editors: Lucinda Dodds and Emma Dobinson
Designer: Redback Publishing

Originated by Redback Publishing

Acknowledgements
Abbreviations: l—left, r—right, b—bottom,
t—top, c—centre, m—middle
We would like to thank the following for permission to reproduce photographs:
Shutterstock; 13tl kiraziku2u / Shutterstock.com, 23 tr FloFid / Shutterstock.com

Manufactured in the United States of America

CPSIA compliance information: Batch #CSENS26: For further information
contact Enslow Publishing LLC, New York, New York at 1-800-398-2504.

Please visit our website, www.enslowpublishing.com.
For a free color catalog of all our high-quality books,
call toll free 1-800-398-2504 or fax 1-877-980-4454.

Cataloging-in-Publication Data
Names: Singer, Warren.
Title: From farm to table / Warren Singer.
Description: Buffalo, NY : Enslow Publishing, 2026. |
Series: On the farm | Includes glossary and index.
Identifiers: ISBN 9781978546011 (pbk.) |
ISBN 9781978546028 (library bound) | ISBN 9781978546035 (ebook)
Subjects: LCSH: Food--Juvenile literature. | Food crops--Juvenile literature. |
Farm produce--Juvenile literature.
Classification: LCC SB1776.U6 S564 2026 | DDC 630.973--dc23

CONTENTS

HAPPY BIRTHDAY!

Vanilla

This beautiful birthday cake came from a bakery, but nearly all the things in it were grown or collected by a farmer on a farm.

Chocolate

Flour

Salt

Milk
Butter
Eggs
Raspberry
Sugar
Nuts

BREAD AND CAKES

The flour we use to make bread, cakes, biscuits, muffins, and ice cream cones comes from grains.

Grains are the seeds of different types of grasses. Farmers grow grains in huge fields. Big machines harvest the seeds. These need to be milled to make them into flour for cooking.

Milling means that the seed is pressed and rolled until the white center becomes a powder that we can use for cooking.

Grains include wheat, rye, barley, oats, rice, and corn.

FACT

Rice is a grass seed, just like wheat.

FACT

Corn is a very large grass seed that grows on a tall, green plant.

FRUIT

Farmers grow fruit in orchards where there are hundreds or even thousands of fruit trees. Fruit is the sweet and juicy flesh that covers the seed of a plant.

Nuts are the seeds of fruit. Almond farmers collect the seeds, but the fruit around them is sour. Very few people like to eat almond fruit.

Watermelon and jackfruit are some of the biggest fruits.

FACT

Dried fruit is sweeter than fresh fruit, and it lasts longer.

FACT

The smelliest fruit is the durian. It tastes good but it smells disgusting.

DID YOU KNOW?
Bananas are the most farmed fruit in the world.

VEGETABLES

Farmers grow vegetables in large fields, or even in small gardens. The parts that we eat are usually the leaves, roots, or branches of plants.

Potatoes are root vegetables that have fed millions of people for thousands of years. Leafy greens include lettuce, cabbage, spinach, and bok choy. They all need a lot of water to grow well.

Sometimes it is hard to tell if a food is a vegetable or a fruit. Vegetables are not as sweet as fruits, and we cook with them more than we cook with fruits.

FACT

Bugs love to eat vegetables, so farmers use chemicals to keep them away.

FACT

There are hundreds more types of vegetables than we see in a supermarket.

DID YOU KNOW?

Carrots were originally white, pale yellow, and purple.

MILK AND CHEESE

Most of the milk products around the world are made with milk from dairy cows. Cows graze on grass or eat hay, then farmers collect the milk.

The cheese on pizzas and in burgers comes from milk. Other milk products that we would not have without farmers are ice cream, yogurt, butter, and even chocolate.

FACT
Some milk also comes from goats, sheep, and camels.

FACT
Soy milk comes from a type of bean.

MEAT

Humans have always eaten meat. We used to have to hunt animals for food, but now most of us buy our meat at the store.

Beef from cattle and meat from sheep are so popular as foods that there are huge farms around the world raising these animals. More are needed every day as the number of humans increase.

Meat and live animals are sent to other countries for food.

FACT

Meat grown in a science lab is a new way to produce food from animals.

FACT

"Meat" made from plants is not real meat, but is made for people who do not like to eat animals.

DID YOU KNOW?
Pork is the most widely consumed meat in the world.

EGGS

Birds naturally lay eggs that can hatch into baby chicks. But the eggs you see at the supermarket don't have baby chicks inside. They come from chicken farms where the eggs are collected for people to cook and eat.

There can be thousands of chickens on a farm. Farmers collect all the eggs, sort them into sizes, and put them in egg cartons. Then the eggs travel in trucks to stores.

People may make eggs into meals for breakfast, lunch, or dinner. They also mix them with sugar to make sweet desserts.

FACT

Farmers feed chickens special food so that their eggshells are strong and do not crack easily.

FACT

The heaviest recorded chicken egg weighed 1 pound (454 g).

FISH

Fish can be farmed in big tanks of water inland, or they might be enclosed in a part of a river or the ocean.

Raising fish on farms makes it easier to catch them when the time comes to sell them as food.

Fish farmers can check that the fish on their farms are growing well and do not have diseases.

FACT
Shrimp, crabs, and oysters can be grown in farms.

FACT
More than half of the world's seafood now comes from farms.

INSECTS

Insects are mainly farmed as food for animals and fish. Cockroaches breed so quickly that they can provide a lot of food for animals in a short time.

Farming insects takes up a small area when compared to farming livestock or growing crops.

Not all insects are good for us to eat, but some are part of people's daily meals in many parts of the world.

Witchetty grubs and crickets can be very tasty if they are cooked in the right way. They are also a healthy food with a lot of protein in them.

FACT

Insects can be very poisonous, so there are only some that we can eat safely.

FACT

Dried maggots (fly grubs) are a great food source for farm animals.

SEAWEED

Seaweed is a plant that farmers can grow in sea water. It's a healthy food source that tastes salty.

Farmers grow seaweed in places where the water is shallow when the tide is out, so they can walk around and look after their crop. When it is ready, they cut it and sell it.

China and Indonesia farm the most seaweed. It is a very popular ingredient in many Japanese meals.

FACT
Seaweed products are added to cans of pet food.

FACT
Some gummy candies are made from seaweed.

BEES

Honey farmers keep thousands of bees to produce honey. They have to take the beehives all around the countryside, looking for places where there are flowers for the bees to feed on.

The female bees fly out from the hive, collecting the flower pollen. They return home in the evening and chew on the nectar converting it to honey, which they store in honeycomb cells.

The waxy honeycomb is spun in a machine to separate it from the delicious honey.

FACT
A honeybee dies after it stings you.

FACT
Beekeepers wear clothes that cover them well so they do not get stung.

HERBS AND SPICES

Even though we only use a tiny amount of herbs and spices in each meal, they are very important for adding extra flavor.

Herbs come from the leaves and stems of plants. Spices come from the bark, seeds, and roots.

Spices make food taste good, and some of them also stop food from going bad.

Saffron is a yellow spice that comes from flowers. It is one of the most expensive spices because it takes so long for a farmer to collect enough for sale.

FACT

In the past, spices used to be used as money.

FACT

Some herbs are strong medicines for all sorts of illnesses.

HOME FARMS

Not all farms are huge, with thousands of animals and enormous areas covered with crops. Some farms are tiny.

At home, people can grow enough food for themselves, or perhaps just a little extra to swap with other gardeners.

Most grow organic food. This means that no chemicals or pesticides are used.

People who have a hobby farm do not need to grow food to survive, but they like to do it, and they enjoy the way of life.

FACT

People used to living in a crowded city often want to have a hobby farm.

FACT

Growing organic food is becoming more and more popular.

UNUSUAL FOODS FROM FARMS

GELATIN

This comes from the bones and skins of animals. We eat gelatin in sweet jellies and preserved meats.

COCHINEAL

This is a red coloring that comes from little insects. Farmers collect and crush them to produce the red color that is used in many foods.

SPIDERS

Huge spiders are a popular snack in parts of Thailand and Cambodia. People farm them in special holes in the ground.

SNAILS

In France, snails are farmed and then sold to restaurants. The meal they make for customers is called escargot.

GLOSSARY

Food from Farms Word List

beehive ... home for bees
crop ... many plants of the same sort grown by a farmer
enclosed ... closing something into an area so that it cannot get out
harvest ... cut or pick a crop
honeycomb ... waxy structure bees make in their beehive
orchard ... place where there are many fruit trees together
organic food ... food grown without added chemicals
pollen ... powdery food bees collect from flowers
preserved ... kept from going bad
protein ... part of food that helps our body to grow
restaurant ... place where people go out to eat
shallow ... not deep
tide ... daily movement of oceans as the level rises and falls

INDEX